I0469856

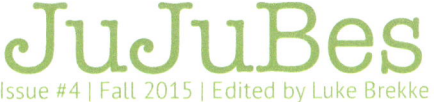

JuJuBes

Issue #4 | Fall 2015 | Edited by Luke Brekke

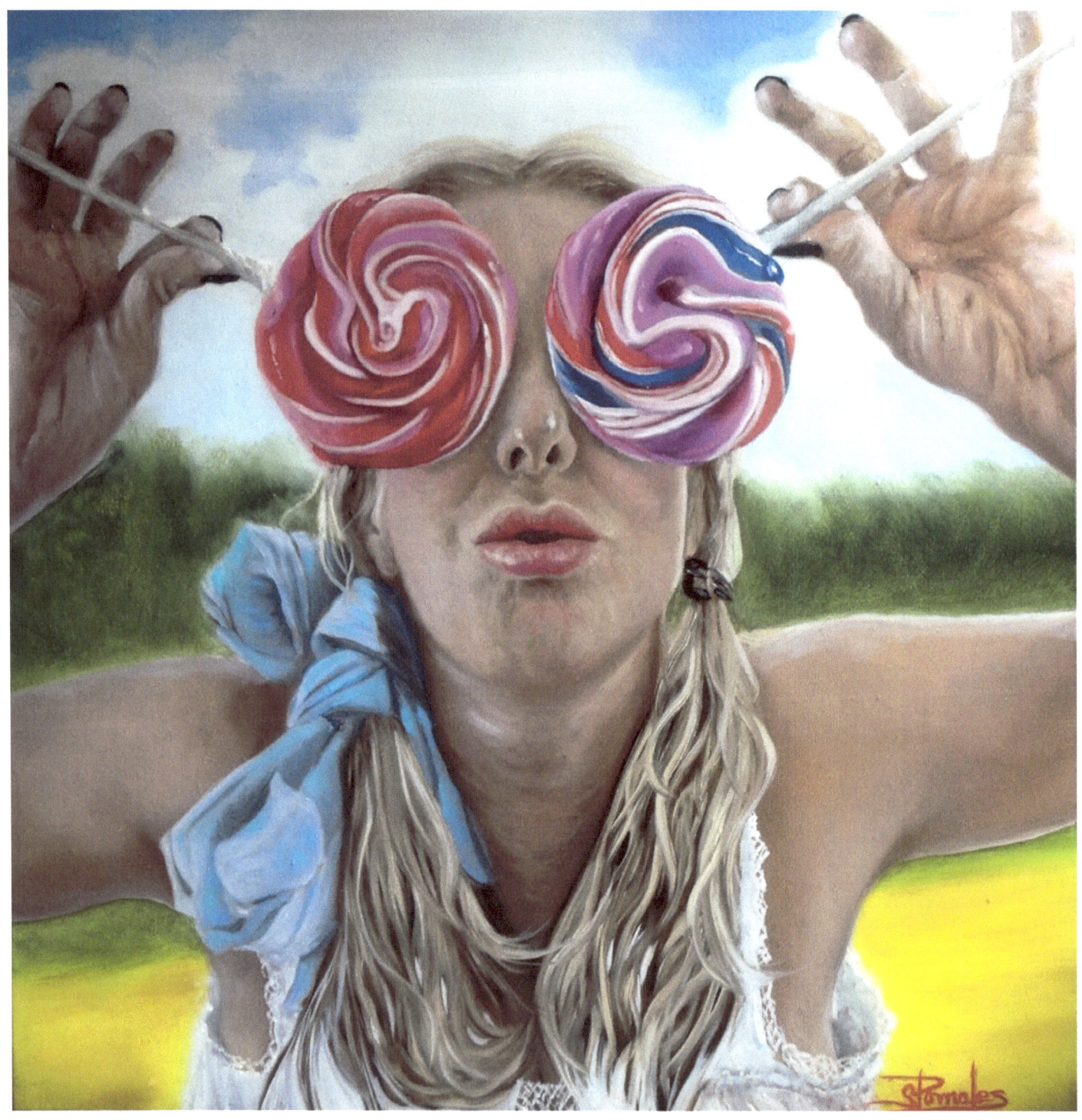

Contributors

art

Sharon Pomales was born and raised in San Juan, Puerto Rico and became interested in art at the age of eight. She studied for a short period at the atelier in Isla Verde of the late Argentinean portrait artist Antonio Gantes. Her father, Raul Pomales-Ledee, a watercolor artist, commercial illustrator and Art Director was also a mentor and teacher until he passed away in Orlando, FL in 2006. Sharon moved to the US in 2012 and lives in Bay Village, OH. Her work is represented by Lovetts Gallery in Tulsa, Oklahoma.

poems

Owen Andrews lives and works in Cambridge, Massachusetts. He received his MA in English from the University of Virginia, where he studied the Puritans, the Transcendentalists, and Henry James. His poems have appeared in *Persephone* and *Epiphany*.

Joseph J. Capista's poems have appeared in *Ploughshares, Slate,* and *Smartish Pace.* He teaches writing at Towson University and lives with his family in Baltimore.

Yuan Changming, 8-time Pushcart nominee and author of 5 chapbooks, grew up in rural China, started to learn English at 19, and published monographs on translation before moving to Canada. With a PhD in English, Yuan currently edits *Poetry Pacific* with Allen Qing Yuan in Vancouver, and has poetry appearing in *Best Canadian Poetry, Best New Poems Online, Threepenny Review* and 1069 others across 36 countries.

Francine Conley has a chapbook, *How Dumb the Stars* (Parallel Press, 2001). Recent poems have appeared or are forthcoming in *American Literary Review, Juked, Paris-Atlantic, Shadowgraph Magazine, Asteri(x) Journal, Naugatuck Review, Hartskill Review*, and *NER*, among others. For more on her art: francineconley.com

Kaisa Edy is a poet and editor who splits her time between Tacoma, Washington and Oxford, England. She has been a work fellow at The Frost Place Poetry Seminar, and attended the Hope Equals Art Residency in Palestine in 2013. Her work has appeared in *Salt Hill Journal*.

Daye Phillippo is a graduate of Purdue University and Warren Wilson MFA for Writers. She is the recipient of The Elizabeth George Grant and a Mortarboard Fellowship for poetry. Her work has appeared or is forthcoming in *Shenandoah, Natural Bridge, The Fourth River, Cider Press Review, Crux, Ruminate,* and others. She lives in a creaky, old farmhouse on twenty rural acres in Indiana with her husband and their youngest son.

David B. Prather received his MFA from Warren Wilson College. His poetry has appeared in several journals, including *Colorado Review, Seneca Review. Poet Lore, Prairie Schooner, ONTHEBUS, American Literary Review,* and others. He currently spends his time as an actor and director at the Actors Guild of Parkersburg.

GOSS183
www.poetsandartists.com
Publisher Didi Menendez

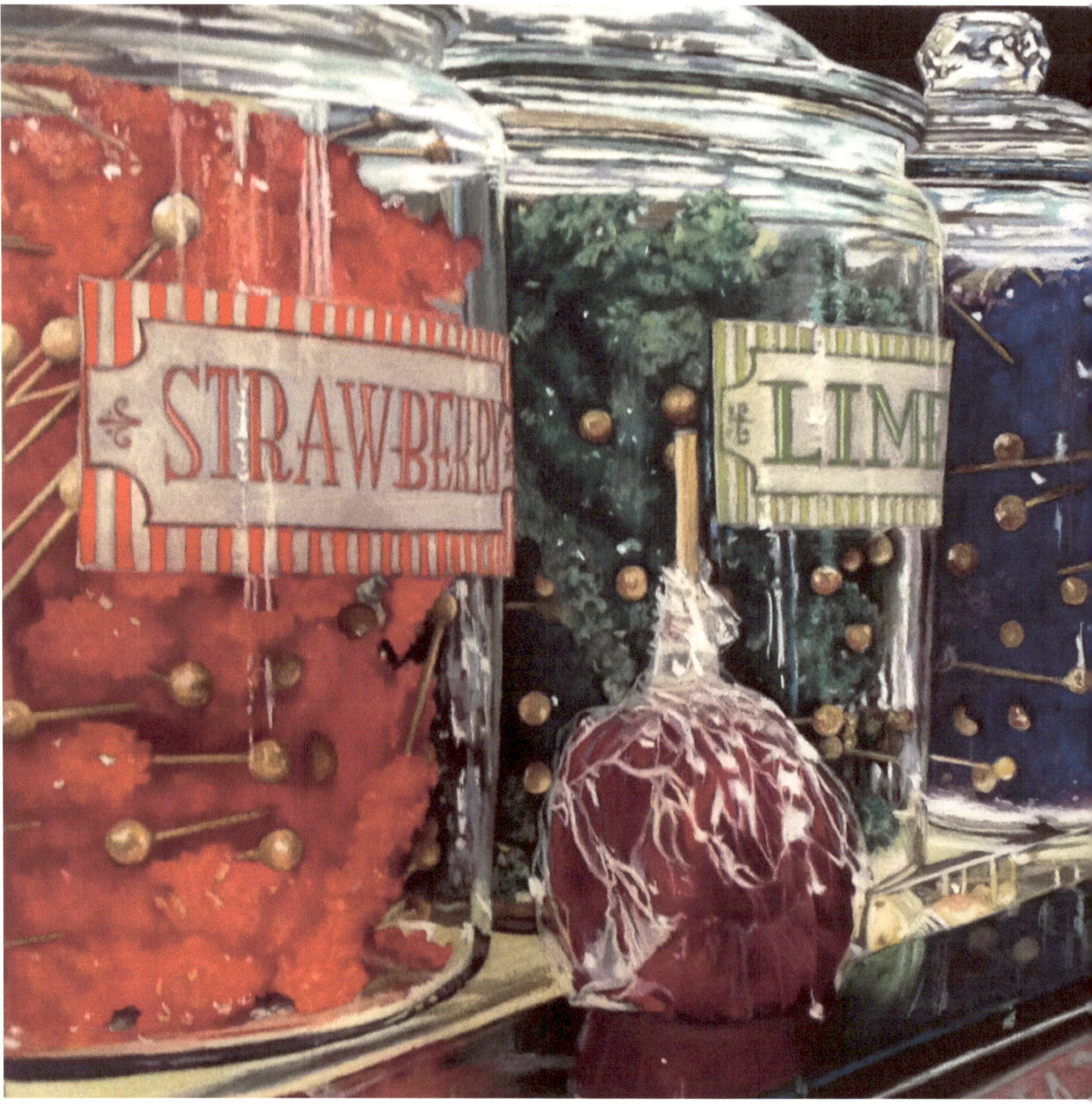

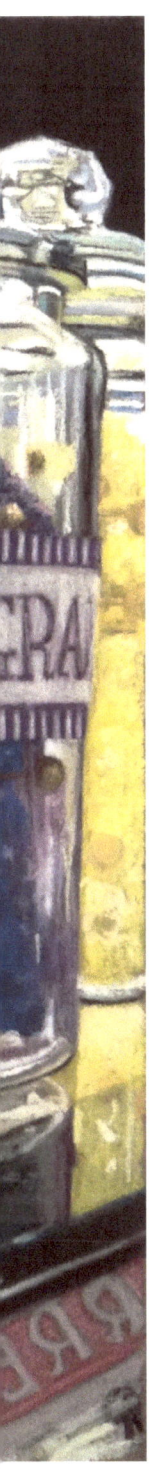

Joseph J. Capista

Light Logic

Time and Space persist
    On canvas, too, as syllogism:

Shade falls we know in shape
    Of truth, not exactly factualism.

Yet, how vexed are we
    As rapt inside this gallery

Some Sunday-looker draws
    Our attention to art's sleight,

Frames the seen as rhetoric
    In which opposing possibility

Possibilitates an opposite, eye
    Rhyme mere stay against

Death's relative darkness,
    Etc. Slantwise, we proceed

Unmoved into an adjacent
    Room in which another

Portrait's glass reflects
    Countenance less radiant

Than we, in our opacity,
    Expect to see amid such

Corresponding beauteous
    Busts, and which we, beyond

All shadow of a doubt,
    Recognize belongs to us.

Vigilante Day Parade

Worst is seeing kids handcuffed
in the cruiser's slick backseat.
After one such group home incident,
I haul our residents, *in loco parentis,*
to Helena's Vigilante Day Parade,
roar along with them at ballot-burning
outlaws, anachronistic flapper floosies,
paper cattle, twine-hanged effigies.
I recognize Cy's mom and watch
the crowd grow tense around her.
She hums a drunk tune on her float-
tossed kazoo then spits on the guy
beside her. He parleys with a fist.
A rookie cop cuffs their wrists
together and radios for back-up
as parents account for their children
and I account for mine—no one's
tried to bolt or fight or even smoke.
But Cy ignores the scene, dives
for candy coins or a plastic badge.
He's too old for this, I think.
Behind the final marching band
trot black-hatted vigilantes, their
whips and Remingtons all action
as they drive demons and hellcats
from our snow-hemmed valley.
Once our day is saved, we cheer.
We came expecting outlaws.
We came expecting justice.

Run Till You Die

We saw it in tin thimbled mothers
and oaken fathers' pocket knives.

But this is about July nights, unseaming
heat and storm clouds sixteen miles off.

Hands aprayer, we parted meadow grass
and entered to run until we half died,

fell with fever's thumbprint on our brow,
one knee buckling after the other.

We called this a game. All glorious fury,
we knew only the world we knew blurred,

our bodies urged by some gnostic velocity
that took us back to origin, back to earth.

And we rose from meadow running,
skin matted with burrs and thistle, yes,

but also hanks of blue stem, red winged
blackbird feather, snake egg, mica fleck,

latticed wing of damselfly—cataracts
thickening against bare and acrid chests.

Still each presses my night-cooled skin;
still each ballast holds me steady as I go.

Yuan Changming

Birds of Varied Feathers: A Confucian Vision

Come, come
You peng from the Zhuangzian northern darkness
You swan from the Horacean meadows
You pheasant from under Li Bo's cold moon
You oriole from Dufu's green willow
You dove from the Dantean inferno
You phoenix from Shakespeare's urn
You swallow from the Goethe oak or
The Nerudan dense blue air, you cuckoo
From the Wordsworthian vale, you albatross
From the Coleridgean fog, you nightingale
From the Keatsian plum tree, you skylark
From the Shelleyan heaven, you owl
From under the Baudelairen overhanging years
You unnamed creature from the Pushkinian alien lands
You raven from near Poe's chamber door
You parrot from the Tagorean topmost twig
And you crows from among my cawing words

Come, all of you, more than 100 kinds of
Birds from every time spot or spot moment

Come, with your light but strong skeletons
Come, with your hard but toothless beaks
Come, with your colored feathers, and flap your wings
Against Su Dong-po's. painting brush strokes

Come, all you free spirits of nature
Let's join one another and flock together
High, higher up towards mabakoola

Ice Chips

I keep waking out of dreams
of beaches, dancers, people I work with.
The window's open; maybe the fresh air
made me dream of running—
just slipping on shorts and taking off.
You've emailed me a poem, and you ask,
did it really snow here, in October?
I see the snow, and sleep some more,
and there is Ken, from school,
in a geometric dance for twelve dancers,
taking all twelve parts. He stops
to take off his shirt, no,
all his clothes, and starts again,
his dancer's buttocks still,
at fifty-plus, as perfect as a boy's.
In my fifties I have lost my way
in love's wood and sleep alone.
No "sex at dawn" (a book
a friend is reading, challenging
monogamy on evolutionary grounds)
for me, just poems from the other,
snow-free coast, and a cool breeze
like the ice chips patients
in the ICU get when they're intubated
and their mouths are dry.
You don't know how good
those chips are—better than anything.

May Sun

It hurts to be inside today.
Our work, to keep us here,
must matter to the race,
the world, the future.

Outside, a longed-for spring
(however cramped by buildings,
sidewalks, roads) forces
its business, making do.

Trees' green flowers open
by a lab where engineers
devise robotic bees
in case we lose the real ones—

a thought as hard and bright
as May sun on a truck hood
in a hundred-acre parking lot
along a ten-lane road.

"The trouble with our time
is that the future isn't
what it used to be."
Pollen silvers the horizon.

In this sudden heat,
maples, pines, and oaks
release their pollen all at once.
Did they used to do that?

My teenage son could care less.
"What's this, governance by anecdote?"
is how a CEO might put it.
Statistics are the Latin of our time.

Holy Crap

Sea-tang over doctored elms,
far from seaweed's confusion,
softens an hour adrift
in traffic's fusillades.
Music, t-shirts, hip-bones
ally with ocean edges on the side
of pleasure, as clouds, elbows,
windbreakers never will.
To sustain anything—a note,
an attitude, an empire—requires
a type of lucid dreaming; by dreaming
we mean feeding on the source code
of flowers, light snow, warm rain,
kisses (soft and hard) and all
the syllabus of love. For the forlorn,
caught in the trap of days
like other days, and summer's failing,
that text washes out in cold rain,
or tears; the stony peninsula
narrows ahead, as pursuers
in sensible outerwear—dentists,
probably—get closer.

Tobacco Past

He spit Virginia out like tobacco,
sick of witnessing drink's raised fist.
At fourteen, slammed the door,
struck out on his own.
In every good story, tragedy
eventually asks for a map,
secures a mode of transporation,
heads for the home imagined
where there's work, a hot meal
that ends with apple pie baked
by a good woman who smiles
behind a hospital switchboard, waits
rose-among-thorns, as he called her,
to be wooed into bloom.
But early memories crowd the rose garden
like crabgrass sprung up in tobacco
from roots not rooted out,
blades that amaze with their vigor.
He strikes with the hoe's sharp edge,
builds a pyre of forgetting
so that when his children ask
about his tobacco past, a clean field,
a charred silence in place of relatives.
And when he grows weary
with secret-keeping, he keeps up
his strength playing saxophone or clarinet,
tunes like Louis Armstrong's
"On the Sunny Side of the Street"
swinging out from the back room.

I used to walk in the shade, baby,
with those blues on parade,
(like any lonely traveler,
soles worn through to soul)
but I'm not afraid, baby.
My rover. . . crossed over
to the sunny side of the street!

Wren

Through the porch door propped open for the cat, a wren.
Tiny terrified pulse and flutter
among the clutter — plants, tools, muddy shoes,
the tumble of cardboard boxes.
You wing — window ledge to electric cord dangling
from the heat lamp clamped to a shelf.
Not there, little one! If the cat . . . .
You fly up into the plate glass, hard!
Fall back to the window ledge, upright, but stunned.
Stub of tail splayed for balance,
breathing fast through little open scissors of dark beak.
Above each eye, thin brushstroke of white, streak
drawn back to the body's throb,
warm, reddish brown feathers.
Your small round eye blinking, blinking
as if to ask why or where or who
would leave open a door, invite a wren
in to such an unwrenlike space
and how to escape, escape?
O, little native! Blunderer through doors intended
for others, I empathize.
This plate glass dilemma, storefront display,
promise of burning bush and maple, spirea and sky,
but, no. As if wind and rain and mate,
and where to build a nest aren't enough.
I hinge open the door, wide as it will go.
You collect yourself long minutes,
then hop out across the table, wing away. . . .
All summer long, each liquid *tea-kettle, tea-kettle,*
                              tea-kettle, tea-kettle, tea will be you.

Original Sin

I am born in a chest of drawers
where I sleep among t-shirts and underthings.

My sister is born in a laundry basket
with clothes fresh from the dryer.

My mother tumbles into creation
in a shack on a gentle slope

where the morning sun barely touches
the tops of sycamore trees.

And my father springs from rain water
puddled in a tire rut along a dirt road

where he metamorphoses
with tadpoles and changeling bugs.

If this sounds like mythology, it is. It is
a flash of light at the beginning of time.

It is a swirl of ethos and pathos
and origin and entropy.

It is June bugs and Japanese beetles,
tent worms and zebra swallowtails.

It is a cryptic emergence from a quiet chrysalis.
Let me belabor the point.

I have what is commonly known as a touchstone,
literally a stone boulder tucked into Standing Stone creek.

This is not the namesake of the stream, though
it looks like a reason for sudden diversion.

This is where I learn to swim,
held lightly in my father's arms.

This is where I hook sunfish and bluegill
with bread and cheese molded to the barb.

This is the education of gods, or so I am told,
all frivolity and fantasy. Stormy afternoons

in August, clouds a sickly amber and charcoal
push back sunlight with sheets of rain

while floods encroach upon fields
of swagger grass and falderal flowers.

Take my word. I speak the gospel.
Look around, and you will see

the devastating creation of the universe.
Close your eyes to the light. Yes.

I will lead you astray
when you need to be led astray.

I will lead you down the garden path
to pluck the herbs of solidarity and eternity.

Francine Conley

So Long As Muskrat Distracts I Will Not Interpret What I See

1. Muskrat is an earth diver. He circles shorelines for thawed silt clumps he pushes up into a mound. Grasps what he can in his jowls, gnaws on dried cattails, grips stems in his claws, deposits the rot mustered into a divine heap, an ugly heart.

2. Muskrat goes about his musky business, burrows, drags wetland dregs, transplants muck one spot to the next. Unfettered by a storm he disappears and reappears in the lake's middle, afloat like a broken log. Stilled, the mound built from dregs turns me into something heaped, like joy.

3. Above is a gray sky I want to call filthy, maybe sacred, but I refrain. Unbeknownst to the muskrat a baby eagle drops from a nest, wings outstretched.

4. Comes the roughness of skin, our nakedness a mound touching cold air, bare feet clasped, layers abandoned, limbs outstretched, hair tangled into a shape like violence, love almost felled, the sharp-ness of teeth touching broken as the glass nicked off the shelf.

5. As I watch him move, it's not the muskrat's attention I need. It's his methodology.

6. The storm comes, greets willows that bend and twist. Muskrat gone under, he burrows there, in a place not called heart.

7. Untethered, a mound can float away in a flood. There is no more than stone and dirt and decayed sumac stuffed in his jowls. Now he turns his attention toward me. I don't think adjective, so I name him *him*, sky *sky* and the ground *ground*. Other measurements I give up to risk.

8. Love is as mustkrat dives into earth—as sky, mound, as you, me, as eagle, clouds ransacked and emptied of their form.

9. The eagle knows the luxury of air. So do I.

10. To be so free we can fall and pretend it's like flying.

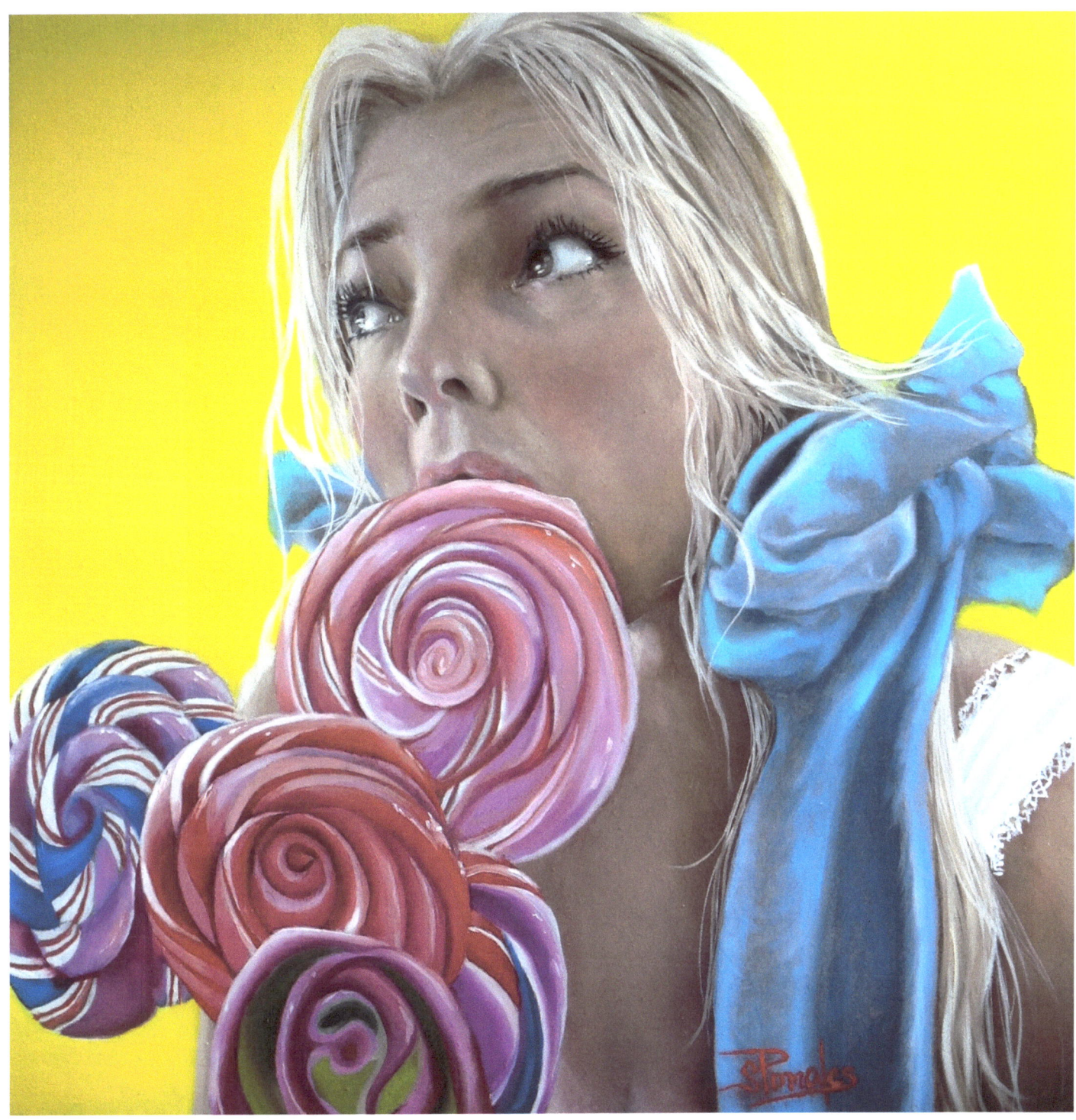

Digitalis Purpurea

Not knowing the wells were full of poison,
we lapped the gathering sweetness—stamens parted,
grainy ovaries embedded in our nails—
each finger covered by a fuchsia mouth,
the slick nectar collecting in our palms.
Your shape blurred behind the light-struck halo
as I sucked the flowers from your fingertips.

Rumex Crispus

But we would pluck only the heads,
the thin, multi-webbed stalks were left to root.
Dipping the crowns in cane sugar,
we boiled them until the water turned
mahogany and sweet, then skimming
the tough pods and clotted remains
from the juices, we would pour
the steaming liquid into cups, and drink—
this is how I made you, she said.

Trillium Erectum

Each part is like the trillium:
small corpus of birthroot, the petals extending
to the point of convex, violet ascending
the carmine folds. Like this flower,
you are hidden and unsought, the rankness building,
and yet, I wonder what you will bear
—what kind of fruit, if any?

Rhinanthus Minor

The call of the terminal raceme:
its fruit enclosed in the coffin-like capsule
is a ripeness mimicking death.
How often I imagined this—the Yellow Rattle,
so easily broken, so effortlessly tilled until forgotten,
but the ground must be scored
before settling the seed inside;
and then, in spring, a cicatrix of blossoms.

Crocus Longiflorus

And after, I pictured crocuses—
the cupped purple translucent against the light,
the swollen ovary hidden beneath
yellow dusted anther, filament
delicate like capillaries, each one
solitary and untangled. In the morning,
the frost would weigh the petals down,
folding into itself, a crocus
cautious in the half-light.

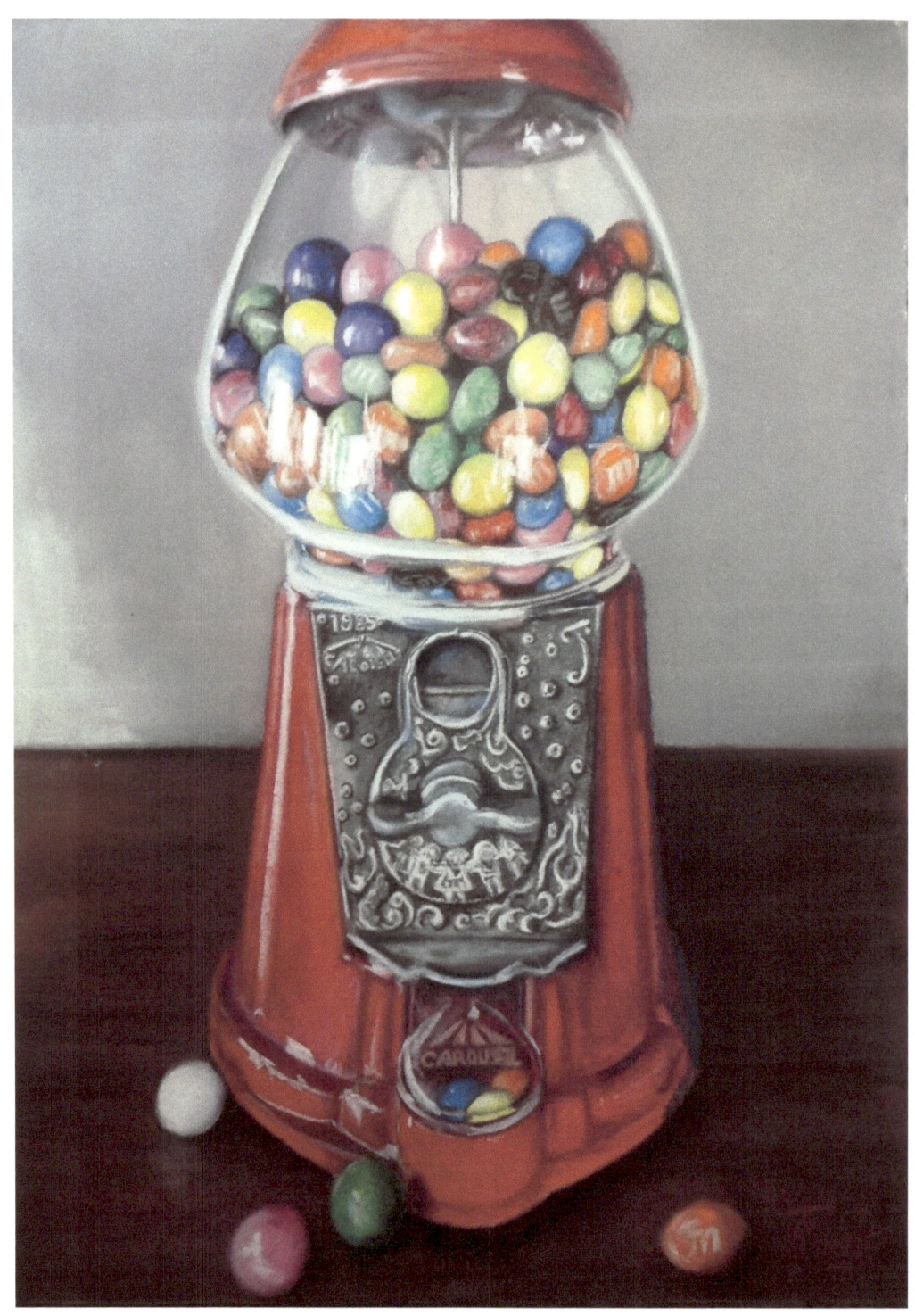

We like danger in poetry. There is a pleasure that is a derivative of speed, of heights, of the forbidden, and those same thresholds quicken our pulse in poems. "My Life had stood - a Loaded Gun -" Dickinson begins her poem, and the surprise of her metaphor and its implications of violence and volatile latency reverberate through the poem as if something had indeed been shot through it. Like all forces in poetry, what constitutes danger in a poem is always contextual. The blatantly violent and aggressive may not unnerve us nearly so well as those dangers we cannot quite name yet perceive as tremors, as plain evidence of something working below the surface. An invisible worm, a figure that seems wholly impotent, is a noxious agent of corruption in Blake's "The Sick Rose." In Kaisa Edy's suite of poems that appears in this issue, danger is a constant feature. Each of the five poems takes its title from the Latin name of a flower and unfolds around this ostensible center, yet the language of the poems pushes beyond mere description into weedier, more interesting spaces.

It is dangerous to write poems about flowers—make no mistake. We are suspicious of beauty, not wanting to be duped, and Edy's poems are made striking, in part, by the degree to which they embrace this danger and the means they use to resist it.

> Each part is like the trillium:
> small corpus of birthroot, the petals extending
> to the point of convex, violet ascending
> the carmine folds. Like this flower,
> you are hidden and unsought, the rankness building . . .

The language here is at once precisely accurate and suggestive. The opening phrase tells us that what we are seeing is "like the trillium," meaning it is *not* the trillium, inviting us to read this description of a "birthroot . . . extending . . . ascending" as something else. Yet "birthroot" is another, older name for the *trillium erectum*, or red trillium, a distinct species from the *trillium grandiflorum* (white trillium), so the comparison being made is, after all, only between two species of flowers. That is, until the second sentence, at which point the speaker does compare the flower to the poem's "you," selecting more neutral modifiers (hidden, unsought) and focusing on the wonderfully surprising quality of "rankness." It's this turn in the fifth line that most strenuously resists the danger of writing ornate poetry about flowers. We register a change in diction—a shift from the refined elegance of Latinate words that crowd the poem's first few lines (corpus, extending, convex, violet, ascending) to the wholly Germanic roots of the fifth line (hide, seek, rank, build). We also recognize those potentially negative qualities as something the speaker identifies with the "you," understanding that the speaker is both attracted to and guarded against the person she addresses.

These are not, after all, poems about flowers. "Digitalis Purpurea," the poem that opens the series, shares its title with a work by Italian poet Giovanni Pascoli. Pascoli's is "a poem about the destructive powers of sexual passion," and Edy's poem introduces the same theme. [1] The language is highly tactile, the point of focus extremely close, so we take our bearings from an anatomy of flowers that is highly synonymous with that of humans, and highly suggestive.

> [We] lapped the gathering sweetness—stamens parted,
> grainy ovaries embedded in our nails—
> each finger covered by a fuchsia mouth . . .

Again, the descriptions both attract and repel: there is a grittiness and violence in those "grainy ovaries," something seductive and silenced in that "fuchsia mouth." And there's more at work here. The *digitalis purpurea*, or foxglove, is poisonous. When consumed by humans in small doses, its chemical compound cardiac glycoside digitoxin works as a heart stimulant. When ingested in only slightly higher doses, it is fatal. The danger in Edy's poem, like Pascoli's, is losing oneself to the intoxicating "poison" of desire. By the end of this first poem, the speaker's vision is "blurred" and she sees the one she desires behind a "light-struck halo." This same danger haunts every poem in the series: to be overtaken by what is sensually pleasing, or worse, to give oneself over to someone else.

The textures of the poems themselves threaten at times to overwhelm us, but Edy's descriptions are vivid, not ornate. The difference is critical. In "Rumex Crispus," for example, she describes boiling floral crowns down to a tea, and the act becomes mythical, ending with an unspecified voice saying, "this is how I made you." And yet the action is rendered with such crisp accuracy (through verbs and participles: "pluck," "dipping," "boiled," "skimming") and the details are surprisingly fresh, and rough (the "tough pods and clotted remains"). In this way, the poem resists the more conventional preference for what is "mahogany and sweet," that is, beautiful and pleasing. In "Rhinanthus Minor," Edy describes the flower's "fruit enclosed in the coffin-like capsule" as "a ripeness mimicking death," asserting that "the ground must be scored" before any growth may occur. This recognition of the role of death in the life cycle likewise tempers the poem. It's through lines like these that Edy's poems hazard their course; her clear vision and controlled diction preventing them from becoming sentimental.

Throughout all the poems, we also sense the precariousness of their subject, the delicate unfolding of intimacies only partially disclosed:

> And after, I pictured crocuses—
> the cupped purple translucent against the light
> the swollen ovary hidden beneath
> yellow dusted anther, filament
> delicate like capillaries, each one
> solitary and untangled. . . .

1 Horne, P. R. "Introduction, Notes and Vocabulary." In Selected Poems. Giovanni Pascoli. 156. Manchester University Press. 1983.

These lines, from the final poem in the series, describe the structure of a crocus, but they also point to the structure or method of the poem itself, of each of these poems: that they suggest more than they reveal, the narrative thread always "hidden beneath" the lyric beauty of the poems, and that each of them, though working together, maintains its own "solitary and untangled" function. These poems, in the end, do not have to be read as a series—each sufficiently stands on its own—yet we are invited to read them as one. If we do take these poems as a unified whole, we intimate a story of attraction, deepening intimacy, vulnerability, consummation and birth. Not a new story by any means and, therefore, another danger. It's Edy's handling of her material, once more, that makes us willing to listen to her tell this old story again. Each of these poems rewards the same precise, voracious attention it consistently demonstrates. In the lines above, for instance, tracing the sonic textures reveals an intricate layering of consonance and assonance (*ps* and *cs* alternating through "pictured crocuses—/the cupped purple," for instance, or the long *os* sounding through "swollen ovary" and "yellow"). Looking closely, we also appreciate the way Edy's lines and syntax marshal out the dramatic event of the poem, the way each line ending effectively breaks up the syntax, sometimes at grammatical pauses and sometimes not, but always in a way that directs our attention, that holds our gaze to something common and remarkable unfolding before us.

We like danger in poetry, but we also like control, expertise. Edy's poems provide us with both. They are at once revealing and veiled, by turns lush and clipped. They succeed because they understand exactly what they risk—sentimentality, beauty, convention—and find the means to make us feel along with them, to be captivated and surprised.

www.ingramcontent.com/pod-product-compliance
Lightning Source LLC
Chambersburg PA
CBHW050437180526
45159CB00006B/2565